YESHUA?

DISCOVERING THE JEWISH MESSIAH

BY

THE JEWISH INSTITUTE.com

Copyright©2013 All Rights Reserved

ISBN:978-1492101109

Published by The Jewish Institute.com

Contributing Authors

Ben Solomon (Shlomo) PhD

Al Garza Th.D, PhD

Arthur E. Glass

Printed in the United States of America 2013

TABLE OF CONTENTS

Rabbi's Said What?..pg.5
    The Traditional View……………………..…pg.6
    The Messianic View…………………………pg.9
    The Promise To Eve……………………….…pg.9

Messiah Son of Who?..pg.13

Messiah Who?...pg.22
    When Will The Messiah Come?............................pg.23
    Who Is The Messiah?...pg.26
    54 Reasons Yeshua Is The Jewish Messiah………pg.27

The Name Jesus……………………………………pg.34

Yeshua In Ancient Hebrew………………………pg.40
    The Aleph And The Taw……………………..pg.48
    What Is Truth?...pg.49
    Yeshua Is The Direct Object………………….pg.51
    Yeshua Is The Strong Sign……………………pg.52
    The Taw……………………………………….pg.52
    The Message………………………………..pg.58
    The Taw: Jewish And Christian Scholars……….pg.64

A Former Rabbi Speaks……………………….…pg.70

References………………………………………pg.75
Bibliography……………………………………pg.77
Simple Book Resources……………………………..pg.81

RABBI'S SAID WHAT?

People long for perfection in an imperfect world and for vindication of the righteous in a world of righteousness. This is a basic ingredient of the human heart, mind, and spirit. The whole Tenach[1] is full of this conviction. The prophets of Israel were vehement in denouncing perversion and injustice. While looking forward to the time when a:

"King shall reign in righteousness and princes shall rule in justice. And a man shall be like a hiding place from the wind and a covert from the tempest; like rivers of water in a dry place, like the shadow of a great rock in a weary land[2]"

How is this longing for perfection to be fulfilled? The biblical view taught by the prophets was that Messiah would accomplish it. The prophets foretold a time when Messiah would make final atonement for the sins of both Jew and Gentile[3]. The Hebrew word Mashiach (Messiah) means, *"the Anointed One"* and relates to the One whom Elohim chose to redeem his people. The Tenach teaches that this *"go'el* (kinsman redeemer) shall come to Zion, and unto those who

---

[1] The Tenach is a short hand reference for the Holy Scriptures, consisting of the Books of Moses, the Prophets and the Writings.

[2] Isaiah 32:1-2

[3] E.g., Isaiah 52:15- 53:12; Daniel 9:24-26

turn from transgressions in Jacob."[4] The prophecies inspired by the Ruach Hakodesh (the Holy Spirit) reveal that Israel and mankind will be redeemed by faith in Messiah.

The Traditional Views

Orthodox rabbis of past centuries considered Messiah to be the center of the whole creation. The Messiah is discussed in the context of the "light" in the Genesis creation account."[5] According to the Rabbis, this special light was created before the sun, moon and stars. The Yalkut, a rabbinic medieval anthology, says:

'And Elohim saw the light, that it was good.' This is the light of Messiah ... to teach you that Elohim saw the generation of Messiah and His works before He created the universe, and He hid the Messiah ... under His throne of glory. Satan asked Elohim, Master of the Universe: 'For who is this Light under Your Throne of Glory?' Elohim answered him, 'It is for ... [the Messiah] who is to turn you backward and who will put you to scorn with shamefacedness.' [6]

In another rabbinic reference we are told that: All the prophets who prophesied have only made predictions regarding the Messiah. As regards eternity, it is said in Isaiah 64:4,

---

[4] Isaiah 59:20

[5] Genesis 1:4

[6] Yalkut on Isaiah 60; see Alfred Edersheim. The life and Times of Jesus the Messiah (Wm. B. Eerdmans 1977) p. 728.

'neither hath eye seen, O Elohim, beside Thee, what He hath prepared for him who waiteth for Him.[7]

The rabbis also were aware the Tenach predicted that Messiah would be both humiliated and exalted. They tried to resolve this apparent contradiction in three different ways. The first possibility developed in the Talmud was that Messiah existed from before: the creation of the world and came to earth when the Second Temple was destroyed. Rabbi Shemuel bar Nehmani said: On the day when the Temple was destroyed Israel suffered much for their sins.... And from whence do we know that on that day [when the Temple was destroyed] Messiah was born? For it is written, 'Before she travailed, she brought forth' [the Messiah].[8]

Various reports are then offered as to his whereabouts after his birth. The Babylonian Talmud says that He sits "at the gates of the city of Rome" and suffers affliction with his people. There he awaits Elohim call to step out as exalted Savior and bring about Israel's salvation. He will do it as soon as Israel hears Elohim voice and repents.[9] This view eventually was abandoned, perhaps because it too closely resembled the view of Jewish believers in Yeshua(Jesus), who believed that the Messiah had first come as Suffering Savior and would return in glory as King-Redeemer.

---

[7] Sanhedrin 99a; Berachot 34b; Shabbat 63a

[8] Bereshit Rabbati 133 (Isaiah 66:7)

[9] Sanhedrin 98a

A second explanation of the seemingly contradictory portrayals of Messiah as one both humiliated and exalted appears elsewhere in the Talmud. R. Alexandri said that R. Joshua bar Levi combined the two paradoxical passages; the one that says. *'Behold, one like the Son of Man came with the clouds of heaven'* (Dan. 7:13) [showing Messiah's glory] and the other verse that says, *'poor and riding upon a donkey'* (Zech. 9:9) [showing Messiah's humility]. He explained it in this manner: If they are worthy, He will come 'with the clouds of heaven;' if they are unworthy He will come 'poor and riding upon a donkey.'[10]

A third solution is found in the Babylonian Talmud.[11] Here, the two different roles of Messiah are fulfilled in two different Messiahs. The first one is Messiah-Ben Joseph who fights, suffers extreme humiliation, and is pierced, fulfilling Zechariah's prophecy, *"They shall look unto Me whom they have pierced."*[12] The second one is Messiah Ben David, who comes later and to whom Elohim says:

"I will declare the decree, YHWH hath said unto me. Thou art my Son, this day have I begotten thee. Ask of me, and I shall give thee the nations for thane inheritance"[13]

---

[10] Ibid.

[11] Sukkah 52b

[12] Zechariah 12:10

[13] Psalm 2:7

The Messianic View

The rabbis failed to recognize one other possibility -- which the Messiah was to atone for the sins of the people first and then return as the Exalted One to establish his Kingdom. This view, of course inevitably leads to Yeshua (Jesus) as the Messiah, a truth that escaped the rabbis of past and present supported by the Tenach. This view resolves the dilemma faced by most Talmudic rabbis. The rabbis strove to resolve the two distinct threads of prophecies in the Tenach. As a man standing afar off looking at two mountain peaks in direct line, they were unable to discern the "time gulf" that existed between those peaks. With the hindsight of a quarterback and the additional revelation of the Brit Hadasha (New Covenant) the theory which best resolves the paradox is that one Messiah was to come in two different eras for two distinct purposes. He was to come first as the Suffering Savior to atone for the sins of the people and to bring peace to those who repented and received the atonement in faith. He is to come next as the Exalted King to rein judgment upon the unjust and to establish his Messianic Kingdom forever. With this model in mind, it is appropriate to begin to identify this Messiah promised to Eve, in the beginning.

The Promise to Eve

The first ray of promise to redeem mankind is found in the first few pages of the Tenach in the Book of Bereshit.[14] This redemption prophecy was given after the great disaster that overtook our first

---

[14] Genesis 3:15

ancestors. The *"ancient Serpent,"* sometimes called *nahash ha-kadmoni,* was more subtle than any other creature and proved irresistible to Eve, and then to Adam.

Elohim gave Adam and Eve virtual free reign in the Garden of Eden. He told them they could eat from every tree but one, warning them that disobedience would produce very harmful consequences. They chose to eat from that tree of knowledge of good and evil anyway, in clear disobedience to Elohim. Instead of trusting their Father, they yielded to the temptation of pride. After all, the Tempter had promised them, *"Ye shall be like Elohim."*[15]

Adam and Eve's misguided challenge to Elohim uniqueness and authority had to be punished. But along with punishment came a blessing and a promise to humanity. The woman, the first to obey Satan instead of Elohim, is told that out of her seed would come the One who will *"bruise the head"* of this Serpent, whom Satan had used to mislead humanity. According to the prophecy Elohim said:

"I will put enmity between thee and the woman and between thy seed and her seed; He shall bruise thy head: and thou shall bruise his heel."[16]

The *"seed of the woman"* would deal a fatal blow to the head of the

---

[15] Genesis 3:5

[16] Genesis 3:15

Serpent. And, the *"seed of the woman"* would in turn sustain a bruise to the heel, a non-fatal blow. The Aramaic paraphrase of the Hebrew Scriptures, Targum Jonathan, relates this Prophecy to the Messiah explaining: But they will be healed [shupf] in the footsteps [heels] in the days of King Messiah.[17] Here, the word shupf is not translated as "bruise" but rather in the sense of "rubbing with a medicine," and thus as "healing." One of the greatest Jewish commentators, 12th-13th century Rabbi David Kimchi, gave support to this Scripture as a prophecy about Messiah's redemption of mankind. He recognized that salvation is by the hand of the conquering Messiah *"who would wound Satan, the head, the king and prince of the house of the wicked."*

How did Eve understand this Scripture? Evidence suggests she understood it to mean that she would bear a child who would "bruise the head of Satan." Note that when Eve bore her first son, Cain, she said, "I have gotten a man from the Lord."[18] The Targum of Palestine elaborates on this verse as follows:

And Adam knew...his wife...and she conceived and brought forth Cain, and she said; 'I have obtained the man, the Angel of the

---

[17] See J.W. Etheridge, The Targum of Onkelos and Jonathan Ben Uzziel on the Pentateuch with the Fragments of the Jerusalem Targum from the Chaldee [hereafter referred to as Etheridge] (Katav 1968) p. 166 vote 8. This targum is commonly referred to as the Targum of Jonathan Ben Uzziel.

[18] Genesis 4:1

Lord.[19]

These verses indicate that Eve expected more than an earthly child, and by her exclamation, one who would literally fulfill the promise. Presumably, when Cain killed Abel her expectations of the *"promised seed"* were dashed. Later, when she finally bore Seth she exclaimed,

"For Elohim has appointed another seed ..." [20]

The rabbis comment on this as follows:

[She (Eve) hinted at] that seed which would arise from another source ... the king Messiah.[21]

Some rabbinic sources, then, did recognize that the Messianic seed would emanate from Eve. When Cain slew Abel, however, Eve realized that Cain - whom Eve had thought was *"the Man"* - was not. Since Abel was dead, he could not qualify either. Thus, the *"Appointed One"* arose from Eve's son, Seth. The genealogical line was now pinpointed.

---

[19] See Etheridge at pp. 169-170.

[20] Genesis 4:25

[21] Midrash Rabbah Genesis 23:5

MESSIAH: SON OF WHOM?

The Messiah was to descend from the seed of Eve, of Seth, of Abraham, Isaac and Jacob, and of Judah and Jesse. The Messianic *"baton"* now passes to Jesse's son David. This is confirmed by the following word spoken by Nathan, the prophet, and directed toward David:

"And when thy days be fulfilled, and thou shalt sleep with thy fathers, I will set up thy seed after thee, which shall all proceed out of thy bowels, and I will establish his kingdom. He shall build a house for my name...." [22]

The immediate cause for this prophecy was David's desire to build a *"house for the YHWH."* He communicated this desire to Nathan, who was inclined to agree that David should build the temple. Nevertheless, contrary to David and Nathan's desire, Elohim spoke through Nathan and said, *"No."* Elohim reasoning for not selecting David to build the Temple was that David was a warrior and had *"shed blood abundantly."* [23] Instead, it was David's son, Solomon, *"the man of Shalom "*(peace), who was destined to build the house of YHWH. Nathan's prophecy, however, extends much farther than the building of an earthly home to house the Ark of Elohim. Nathan continued:

---

[22] II Samuel 7:12-13

[23] I Chronicles 22:8

"I will establish the throne of his kingdom forever. I will be his father and he shall be my son. ... And thine house and thy kingdom shall be established forever before thee" [24] This prophecy did not find fulfillment even in David's son, Solomon. Solomon did not reign as king forever. In fact, Solomon is well known as the king who committed many sins by marrying pagan wives and succumbing to their idolatrous influence.[25]

The eternal throne would be held by Messiah himself, who would establish eternal peace. The prophets, who spoke centuries after David's death, when speaking of the latter days, often invoked the name of David as a reference to this Messiah. For example, the prophet Hosea said,

"Afterward shall the children of Israel return [to their land], and seek YHWH their Elohim, and David their king ... in the latter days."[26]

Since David was no longer alive, it is obvious that the prophet is speaking of the "greater David" - the Messiah. Similarly, YHWH spoke through Ezekiel saying,

"... And I will set up one shepherd over them ... even my servant

---

[24] II Samuel 7:13-14,16

[25] I Kings 11:3-6

[26] Hosea 3:5

David... a prince among them. ..." [27]

The prophet Amos recognized the need to *"raise up the tabernacle of David."* [28] And, of the latter days, the prophet Jeremiah assigned the ineffable name to this Branch of David when he prophesied,

"I will raise unto David a righteous Branch ...and this is the name whereby He shall be called, YHWH Tseidkeynu (YHWH our Righteousness)." [29]

Anyone who read the preceding verse in this text will know that the *"the righteous Branch"* that will be raised up for David is the Messiah. Every scholar both Jewish and non-Jewish will agree that this is a Messianic text. In a book entitled, *"The Messiah Texts: Jewish legends of Three Thousand Years*, he records the following on page 21:

"What is the name of King Messiah? R. Abba bar Kahana said: **"YHWH is his name,** *for it is written, I will raise unto David a righteous shoot....In his days Judah shall be saved....And this is the name whereby he shall be called: The Lord is our righteousness"* [30]

---

[27] Ezekiel 34:23-24

[28] Amos 9:12

[29] Jeremiah 23:5-6

[30] "The Messiah Texts: Jewish legends of Three Thousand Years" by Raphael Patai.

In Chapter 2 of his book he states the following concerning the preexistence and names of the Messiah.

"Others [Jewish Rabbi's] applied to him [the Messiah] the name of God, a daring procedure in the Jewish context."[31]

Finally, the prophet Micah confirms that Bethlehem, the birthplace of David, will also be the birthplace of the *"greater David,"* when he was inspired of the Ruach HaKodesh to speak:

"But thou, Bethlehem Ephra-tah, though thou be little among the thousands of Judah, yet out of thee shall he come forth unto me that is to be the ruler in Israel; whose goings forth have been from of old, from everlasting."[32]

This passage of scripture describes the Messiah who would come and be the ruler of Israel. His going forth from long ago is a reflection of the ancient of days in which the Messiah made his preexistence appearance in history while at the same time, himself being from eternity. *"His goings forth"* in Hebrew is plural and points to a repeated going out and making an appearance. The Hebrew *"Miy-Mei Olam"* describes his origin and dwelling within eternity. He was before all things and he is the creator of all things, so he is Eternal and no part of what was created. Whatever has not

---

[31] The Messiah Texts: Jewish legends of Three Thousand Years, Raphael Patai

[32] Micah 5:2

been created is Elohim.

Also the prophet here could not have been speaking of David since this *"ruler"* is one who was "from everlasting." Also, the prophet speaks of the future and David was dead and buried by the time Micah spoke. The Psalmist, Ethan the Ezrahite, also recognized that the throne referred to in Nathan's prophecy was not simply an earthly throne but one which would be occupied eternally by a *"greater David"*:

I will make him my firstborn, higher than the kings of the earth. ...His seed also will I make to endure forever, and his throne as the days of heaven. ...My covenant will I not break.... I will not lie unto David. His seed shall endure forever, and his throne as the sun before me. It shall be established forever as the moon, and as a faithful witness in heaven.[33]

The Psalmist here is no doubt longing for the *"greater David."* He was expecting a Messiah who would endure forever, and who is Elohim firstborn. A Midrashic portion has this comment about the psalm: Rabbi Nathan said that Elohim spoke to Israel, saying, *"As I made Jacob firstborn for it is written" 'Israel is my son even my firstborn'* (Exodus 4:22), so also will I make Messiah my Firstborn

---

[33]) Psalm 89:27,29,34-37

as it is written; *'I will make him my Firstborn.'* Psalm 89:27)[34]

Accordingly, Messiah is both David's descendant and Elohim begotten Son. This is a most amazing revelation, yet not one that was confined to this psalm. Other scriptures reveal details about the fact of the sonship of the Messiah. Another psalm tells us that Messiah, Elohim begotten Son, will rule the nations and they will worship him; otherwise they will be punished.

"Why do the nations rage... against the Lord, and against his anointed...?... Yet have I set my king upon my holy hill of Zion. I will declare the decree: YHWH hath said unto me, Thou art my Son; this day have I begotten thee."...Kiss the Son, lest he be angry, and yet perish from the way when his wrath is kindled but a little.[35]

Agur Ben Yakeh, one of the writers of a portion of the Book of Proverbs, further identifies Messiah as the Son of Elohim when he poses a riddle:

---

[34] Midrash Rabbah Shemot 19. Jewish commentators interpret the psalmic passage as Messianic. They note rightfully that the faithful witnesses in heaven are the sun and the moon mentioned in the psalm. Hence, they link it to a prophecy in the book of Jeremiah where God takes the sun, moon and stars to be witnesses before him that Israel will endure forever (Jeremiah 31:35-36). These same witnesses testify that Messiah is the first begotten of God and that He will endure forever.

[35] Psalm 2:1-2, 6-7. This warning to obey God's anointed (which is fairly translated Messiah), also here described as Son, is likewise conveyed in the Deuteronomy prophecy previously discussed in Chapter Seven, where the Messiah is described as a prophet "like unto Moses," and "whosoever will not hearken unto my words which he shall speak ... I will require it of him." (Deuteronomy 18:19) The warning also attaches to a scripture in the book of Exodus where the Messiah is revealed as the Angel of the Lord: "Behold I send an Angel before thee to keep thee in the way. ... Beware of him and obey his voice, provoke him not..." (Exodus 23:20-21)

Who hath ascended up into heaven, or descended?...Who hath established all the ends of the earth? What is his name and what is his Son's name, if thou can tell?[36]

The prophet Isaiah who lived several centuries after David also referred to the Son of Elohim who would sit upon the throne of David forever when he said:

"For a Child shall be born unto us, a Son shall be given unto us, and the rule is on His shoulder. And His Name is called Wonder, Counselor, Strong Ěl, Father of Continuity, Prince of Peace. Of the increase of his government and peace there shall be no end, upon the throne of David, and upon his kingdom, to order it, and to establish it with justice and with righteousness from henceforth even forever." [37]

There is not much disagreement among Jewish scholars that this is speaking of the Messiah. The clear understanding of the passage in Isaiah is that the Messiah would hold titles that only YHWH himself could hold. The ancient Jewish Targum of Isaiah inserts the word Messiah into the passage to make it more clearly on who is being spoken of.

"For to us a child is born, to us a son is given...and his name will be

---

[36] Proverbs 30:4

[37] Isaiah 9:6-7

called the Wonderful Counselor, the Mighty God, existing forever, The Messiah in whose days peace shall increase upon us"[38]

Also in Solomon Buber's note we have the following comment:

"The Messiah is called by eight names: Yinnon, Tzemah, Pele ["Miracle"], Yo'etz ["Counselor"], Mashiah ["Messiah"], El ["God"], Gibbor ["Hero"], and Avi 'Ad Shalom ["Eternal Father of Peace"].[39]

The Jewish understanding of these passages according to the Targum and Buber's is that the Messiah would be El and would exist forever. *"Everlasting father"* is an errant translation of the Hebrew ('abî ' ad). The word *"ad"* (eternity) is in the construct state, the normal way Hebrew expresses the possessive- the noun possessed is put into this state. Thus a better translation is *"Father of Eternity"*. Thus Father of Eternity means that this coming Messianic Child is an eternal being, and He is the one who provides eternal life. This can be compared with Isaiah 63:16b:

"...you, O YHWH, are our Father; our Redeemer from of old is your name."[40]

---

[38] Isaiah Targum 9:6

[39] (S. Buber's note, ibid. p. 87)

[40] Isaiah 63:16b

No mere man, or any created being, could possibly fit this description. In reality there is a special idiom in Hebrew called the *"Prophetic Perfect"* this is where a prophet speaks of future events in the perfect form because he has seen them in the future where they have already happened.

Finally, the prophet Daniel *"saw in the night visions"* of the Messianic Son coming *"with the clouds of heaven"* [41]:

"And there was given him dominion, and glory, and a kingdom, that all peoples, nations, and languages should serve him; his dominion is an everlasting dominion which shall not pass away, and his kingdom that which shall not be destroyed." [42]

Messiah was to be the Son of David. He was also to be the Son of Elohim. This concept has puzzled the rabbis from the first century down to this very day. No mere man can be given such divine titles and be served as YHWH himself.

---

[41] Daniel 7:13

[42] Daniel 7:14

MESSIAH WHO?

As a Jew I knew that the secrets of Israel's redemption and the Messianic Days lay hidden in the book of Daniel. I also knew that some of the great Talmudic and post-Talmudic Rabbis had plunged into the study of this book and even descended the hidden secrets of its symbolic signs. The Talmud and Midrash, discussing Israel's redemption, often refer to the book of Daniel as the revealer of the secret time of Messiah's coming. However I was ominously reminded of a warning and a curse pronounced against those who try to figure out the end. The Talmud says:

May they drop who try to figure out the end; for they say, since the time of his [Messiah's] coming has already arrived yet he did not come, therefore he will not come at all.[43]

This extreme condemnation can be understood when the error of Rabbi Akibah designating Bar Kosiba the Messiah is considered: Rabbi Akibah made the inference, from the verse. *'Yet once, it is a little while, and I will shake the heavens, and the earth, and the sea, and the dry land'* (Haggai 2:6), that Simon Bar Kosiba was the Messiah, though he reigned only for two and a half years.[44]

---

[43] Sanhedrin 97b

[44] Ibid.

I was therefore forewarned that the secrets are in the Scriptures, and but that it was dangerous to make assumptions or to figure them out lest we come to the wrong conclusion, as did Rabbi Akibah. The Midrash even states:

"Two men had the end revealed to them; namely Jacob, as stated in Genesis 49: 1, '... that I may tell you what shall befall you in the last days.' and Daniel (12:1, 4), 'And at that time thy people shall be delivered....But thou O Daniel shut up the words....' So even these two men were forbidden to reveal what they knew ..."[45]

When Will Messiah Come?

The study of our greatest sages brought them to the conclusion that if the dates in the Scriptures are correct, then Messiah should have come in the first century of our era, or thereabouts. In a Talmudic portion it is written concerning the timing of the Messianic Age:
The school of Elijah taught:

"The world is to be for six thousand years; two thousand years empty without Torah; two thousand years with Torah; and two thousand years Messianic Times..."[46]

The many Messiahs, who flourished during that period, claiming themselves to be redeemers, were all great disappointments. Finally, Simon Bar Kosiba, whom Rabbi Akibah called "Bar Kochba," came.

---

[45] Midrash Rabbah Gen. 98:3

[46] Ibid.

Though he was active in the first part of the second century, Rabbi Akibah nonetheless adjusted him to the Messianic claim. For the majority of the Jewish people Bar Kosibah was a tragedy and a disappointment. Apart from the loss of tens of thousands of Jews at his defeat in Betar C.E. 135, his activities resulted in untold sufferings for the surviving, Jews. In an eleventh century rabbinic portion, we read:

"Woe, for the salvation of Israel has perished! But a voice came from heaven saying, Elijah, it is not as you think, but He will be 400 years in the great Sea, and eighty years with the Sons of Korah where the smoke ascends, and eighty years at Rome's gate, and the rest of the years He will travel about the great Cities until the end."[47]

In another rabbinic portion, based in part upon a scripture in the book of Lamentations, *["she has none to comfort (Menachem) of all her friends,"]*[48] the name of the Messiah is identified as Menachem Ben Ami-el.[49] Messiah, then, is clearly *"alive and well"* for the last nineteen hundred years, according to these rabbinic writings. His name is Menachem (the Comforter) Ben Amiel (God is with his People). He started to work around the great Mediterranean Sea and went to Samaria (Korah), then Rome and the ends of the world. We

---

[47] B'reshit Rabbati, pp. 130-131; see Raphael Patai, The Messiah Texts p.125.

[48] Lamentations 1:2

[49] Messiah Texts at 26-27, 122-23

may ask: *"Why was He expected during the first century?* Clearly there was a certainty that Messiah had to appear at that period. This conviction was probably based upon the following passages in the book of Daniel:

Seventy weeks (or heptads - weeks of years) are determined upon the people and upon the Holy City, to finish the transgression, and to make an end of sins, and to make reconciliation for iniquity, and to bring in everlasting righteousness, and to seal up the vision and prophecy. and to anoint the most Holy. Know, therefore. and understand that from the going forth of the commandment to restore and to rebuild Jerusalem unto the Messiah, the Prince, shall be seven weeks, and three score and two weeks; the street shall be built again: and the wall, even in troublous times. And after threescore and two weeks shall Messiah be cut off, but not for himself and the people of the prince that shall come shall destroy the city and the sanctuary. And the end of it shall be with a flood, and unto the end of the war desolations are determined.[50]

This revelation was a result of Daniel's prayers given to him by the angel Gabriel to explain the time, substance and circumstance of Israel's redemption. The time embraced was *"seventy sevens."* Within the sixty nine heptads (weeks of years), that is within 483 years, there will be a building up of Jerusalem's streets and canals, though in troublous times. After these 483 years, *"Messiah is cut off,*

---
[50] Daniel 9:24-26

the city of Jerusalem and the Holy Temple will be destroyed by the people of the prince that shall come."

Messiah was to come before the destruction of the Temple. This is the picture that the archangel Gabriel gave to Daniel.

Who is the Messiah?

It was Daniel's prophecy that challenged me many years to consider the Messiah-ship of Yeshua the Nazarene. Rabbinic authorities to whom I consulted said that the reference to Messiah in Daniel's prophecy was to King Agrippa, Herod's descendant, who is called *"Messiah"* here and who was before the Temple's destruction. The term *"Messiah"* is transferred to a carnal king, like Agrippa, or to the unknown Menachem Ben Amiel as recorded in the Midrash. On the other hand, I learned of Yeshua the Nazarene, who was *"cut off"* forty years before the Second Temple was destroyed.

The revelation given to Daniel also deals with the substance and the circumstances of Messiah's activity, *"to finish the transgression, to make an end of sins and to make reconciliation for iniquity and to bring in everlasting righteousness."* In other words, Messiah's death is distinctly connected with the atoning work that the Temple sacrifices were to accomplish, except that it would be a work of completion and fulfillment far greater than any Temple sacrifices could possibly secure. I was thus enabled to lay aside my fears and prejudices and to open the Brit Hadasha (NT) and learn more of him, who, as the Prophet says:

Hath borne our griefs and carried our sorrows; yet we did esteem Him stricken, smitten of God and afflicted. But He was pierced through for our transgressions. He was bruised for our iniquities, the chastisement for our peace was upon him, and with his stripes we are healed.[51]

Yeshua indeed fits perfectly into Daniel's timetable. No one else qualifies; neither King Agrippa nor the mystical Menachem fulfills Daniel's prophecy, Yeshua is the Messiah! He came to give peace to the individual who repents and accepts his atoning sacrifice. He is coming again in might to establish his Kingdom l'olam va 'ed.[52] Amen!

54 Reasons Yeshua is the Jewish Messiah

The Messiah ... MUST ... meet conditions given both in the O.T. (TaNaKh) and in the N.T (B'rit Hadashah)

1. Be the "seed of the woman that would "bruise " or "crush" the serpents "head" Genesis 3:15, Galatians 4:4, I John 3:8

2. Be the "seed of Abraham" Genesis 12:3, Matthew 1:1, Acts 3:25, Gal. 3:16

3. Be the "seed of Isaac" Genesis 17:19; 21:12, Matt. 1:2; Luke

---

[51] Isaiah 53:1-5

[52] forever and ever

3:34, Heb.11:17-19

4. Be the "seed of Jacob" and the "star out of Jacob" who will "have dominion. Gen. 28:14, Nu. 24:17, 19, Mt. 1:2; Luke 3:34, Rev. 22:16

5. Be a descendant of Judah. Genesis 49:10, Matt. 1:2-3, Luke 3:33, Heb. 7:14

6. Be a descendant of David and heir to his throne. 2 Sam. 7:12-13, Is.9:6-7; 11:1-5, Jere.23:5, Mt. 1:1, 6. Acts 11:23, Ro.1:4

7. Have eternal existence. Micah 5:1-2, Jn.11, 14; 8:58 Co.1:15-19, Eph. 1:3-14, Rev. 1:18

8. Be the Son of God. Psalms 2:7, Proverbs 30:4, Matt. 3:17, Luke 1:32

9. Have God's own name, YHVH (Adonia) applied to him
   Is. 9:5-6(6-7), Jere.23:5-6, Romans 10:9, Phil. 2:9-11

10. Come at a specific time, 483 years after the rebuilding of the wall of Jerusalem. Dan. 9:24-26, Mt. 2:1, 16, 19, Lk. 3:1, 23

11. Be born in Bethlehem, in Judah. Micah 5:1(2) Matt.2:1; Lk.2:4-7

12. Be born of a virgin. Isaiah 7:14, Matt.1:18-2:1, Luke 1:26-35

13. Be adored by great persons. Psalms 72:10-11, Matt.2:1-11

14. Be preceded by one who would announce him. Isaiah 40:3-5, Malachi 3:1, Matt.3:1-3, Lk.1:17, 3:2-6

15. Be anointed with the Spirit of God. Psalms 45:8(7) Isaiah 11:2, 61:1, Matt.3:16, J n. 3:34; Acts 10:38

16. Be a prophet like Moses. Deut. 18:15, 18, Acts 3:20-22

17. Have a ministry of binding up the brokenhearted, proclaiming liberty to the captives and announcing the acceptable year of the Lord. Isaiah 61:1-2, Luke 4:18-19

18. Have a ministry of healing Is. 35:5-6, 42:18, Matt.11:5 and throughout the Gospels

19. Have a ministry in the Galilee. Is. 8:23-9:1(9:1-2), Matt. 4:12-16

20. Be tender and compassionate. Isaiah 40:11, 42:3, Matt.12:15, 20, Hebrews 4:15

21. Be meek and unostentatious. Isaiah 42:2, Matt.12:15-16, 19

22. Be sinless and without guile. Isaiah 53:9, I Peter 2:22

23. Bear the reproaches due others. Psalms 69:10, Isaiah 53:12,

Romans 15:3

24. Be a priest. Psalms 110:4, Heb.5:5-6; 6:20, 7:15-17

25. Enter publicly into Jerusalem on a donkey. Zechariah 9:9, Matt. 21:1-11, Mark 11:1-11

26. Enter the Temple with authority. Haggai 2:7-9, Malachi 3:1, Matt.21:12-24:1, Lk 2:27-38, 45-50, John 2:13-22

27. Be hated without cause. Ps. 69:5(4), Isaiah 49:7, Jn. 15:24-25

28. Be undesired and rejected by his own people. Psalms 69:9(8), Is. 53:2, 63:3, Mark 6:3, Luke 9:58, Jn 1:11, 7:3-5

29. Be rejected by the Jewish leadership. Psalms 118:22, Matt. 21:42, John 7:48

30. Be plotted against by Jews and Gentiles together. Psalms2:1-2, Acts 4:27

31. Be betrayed by a friend. Psalms 41:9, 55:13-15(12-14), Matt.26:21-25, 47,50; John 13:18-21, Acts 1:16-18

32. Be sold for 30 pieces of silver. Zechariah 11:12, Matt. 26:15

33. Have his price given for a potter's field. Zechariah 11:13, Matt.

27:7

34. Be forsaken by his disciples. Zechariah 13:7, Matt.26:31,56

35. Be struck on the cheek. Micah 4:14; 5, Matt. 27:30

36. Be spat on. Isaiah 50:6, Matt.26:67, 27:30

37. Be mocked. Ps. 22:8-9(7-8), Matt.26:67-68, 27:31, 39-44

38. Be beaten. Isaiah 50:6, Matt.26:67; 27:26, 30

39. Be executed by crucifixion, by having his hands and feet pierced. Ps.22:17(16), Zech.12:10, Mt.27:35, Lk 24:39, Jn. 19:18, 34-37; 20:28, Rev. 1:7

40. Be thirsty during his execution. Ps. 22:16(15) , John 19:28

41. Be given vinegar to quench that thirst. Ps. 69:22(21), Matt. 27:34

42. Be executed without having a bone broken. Exodus 12:46, Ps. 34:21(20), Jn. 19:33-36

43. Be considered a transgressor. Isaiah 53:12, Matt. 27:38

44. Be "cut off, but not for himself" 69 x7years after rebuilding of the wall of Jerusalem. Daniel 9:24-26, Matthew 2:1, Luke 3: 23

45. Be the one whose death would atone for the sins of mankind. Isaiah 53:5-7, 12, Mark 10:45, Jn. 1:29, 3:16, Acts 8:30-35

46. Be buried with the rich when dead. Isaiah 53:9, Matt. 27:57-60

47. Be raised from the dead. Ps 2:7, 16:10 , Isaiah 53:9-10 Matt. 28:1-20, Acts 2:23-36,13:33-37 , I Cor. 11:4-6

48. Ascend to the right hand of God. Psalms 16:11, 68:19(18), 110:1, Luke 24:51, Acts 1:9-11, 7:55; Hebrews 1:3

49. Exercise his priestly office in heaven. Zechariah 6:13, Romans 8:34, Heb. 7:25-8:2

50. Be the cornerstone of God's Messianic Believing Community. Ps 118:22-23, Is. 28:16, Mt.21:42, Eph.2:20, I Peter 2:5-7

51. Be sought after by Gentiles as well as Jews. Isaiah 11:10, 42:1, Acts 10:45; 13:46-48

52. Be accepted by the Gentiles. Isaiah 11:10, 42; 1-4, 49:1-12 Matt. 12:21, Ro.9:30; 10:20, 11:11; 15:10

53. Be the King. Psalm 2:6, John 18:33, 37

54. Be Seen by Israel as pierced. Zechariah 12:10, Psalm 22:17 (16), Luke 24:39, John 19:34-37, Revelation 1:7

*Courtesy of David Stern, *Complete Jewish Bible*.

THE NAME JESUS
Arthur E. Glass

In dealing with my Jewish brethren for the past many years in Canada, the United States, Argentina, and Uruguay, I had one great difficulty, and it was this: My Jewish people would always fling at me this challenging question, "If Jesus is our Messiah, and the whole Old Testament is about Him, how come His name is never mentioned in it even once?"

I could never answer it satisfactorily to their way of thinking, and I admit I often wondered why His name was not actually written in the Old Bible. Oh, yes, I could show them His divine titles in Isaiah 7:14, 9:6 and Jeremiah 23:5, 6, and even the word MESSIAH in several places; but the Hebrew name that would be equal to Jesus, that I could not show. Then one day the Holy Spirit opened my eyes, and I just shouted. There was the very NAME, Jesus, found in the Old Testament about 100 times all the way from GENESIS to HABAKKUK! Yes, the very word - the very NAME - which the angel Gabriel used in Luke 1:31 when he told Mary about the Son she was to have. "Where do we find that NAME?" you ask. Here it is, friend: Every time the Old Testament uses the word SALVATION (especially with the Hebrew suffix meaning "my," thy," or "his"), with very few exceptions (when the word is impersonal), it is the very same word, YESHUA (Jesus), used in Matthew 1:21. Let us remember that the angel who spoke to Mary and the angel who spoke to Joseph in his dream did not speak in

English, Latin, or Greek, but in Hebrew; and neither were Mary or Joseph slow to grasp the meaning and significance of the NAME of this divine Son and its relation to His character and His work of salvation. For in the Old Testament all great characters were given names with a specific and significant meaning.

For example, in Genesis 5:29, Lamech called his son "Noah [Comfort], saying, *This same shall comfort us concerning our work and tell of our hands.*" In Genesis 10:25, Eber calls his firstborn son, "*Peleg [Division]; for in his days was the earth divided.*" The same is true of Abraham, Sarah, Isaac, Jacob (changed to Israel-God's Prince), and all of Jacob's sons (see Genesis, chapters 29-32). In Exodus 2:10, Pharaoh's daughter called the baby rescued from the Nile, "*Moses [Drawn-Forth]: and she said, because I drew him out of the water.*" And so we can go on and on to show the deep significance of Hebrew names.

Now then, when the angel spoke to Joseph, husband of Mary, the mother of our Lord, this is what he really said and what Joseph actually understood: "*And she shall bring forth a son, and thou shalt call his name Jesus [YESHUA (SALVATION)]: for he shall save [or salvage] his people from their sins*" (Matthew 1:21). This text was so forcibly brought home to my soul soon after I was converted over 24 years ago, that I saw the whole plan of the Old Testament in that one ineffable and blessed NAME.

So let us proceed to show clearly the Hebrew name YESHUA (Greek = Iesus: English = Jesus) in the Old Testament.

When the great Patriarch Jacob was ready to depart from this world, he by the Holy Spirit was blessing his sons and prophetically foretelling their future experiences in those blessings. In verse 18 of Genesis 49 he exclaims, *"I have waited for thy salvation, 0 Lord!"* What he really did say and mean was, "To thy YESHUA (Jesus) I am looking, 0 Lord"; or, "In thy YESHUA (Jesus) I am hoping (trusting), Lord!" That makes much better sense.

Of course YESHUA (Jesus) was the One in Whom Jacob was trusting to carry him safely over the chilly waters of the river of death. Jacob was a saved man, and did not wait until his dying moments to start trusting in the Lord. He just reminded God that he was at the same time comforting his own soul.

In Psalms 9:14, David bursts forth, *"I will rejoice in thy salvation."* What he actually did say and mean was, *"I will rejoice in (with) thy YESHUA (Jesus)."*

In Psalm 91:14-16 God says, *"Because he hath set his love upon me, therefore will I deliver him: I will set him on high [raise him above circumstances], because he hath known my name. He shall call upon me, and I will answer him: I will be with him in trouble; I will deliver him and honor him. With long life [eternal life] will I satisfy him, and show him my [YESHUA (Jesus)] salvation."*

Of course, that promise is realized in Revelation 22:3, 4: *"And there shall be no more curse: but the throne of God and of the Lamb shall be in it: and his servants shall serve him: And they shall see HIS face."*

In Isaiah 12:2, 3 we have something wonderful. Here SALVATION is mentioned three times. The reader will be much blessed by reading these glorious verses in his Bible, but let me give them as they actually read in the original Hebrew with Jesus as the embodiment and personification of the word SALVATION:

"Behold, might (or, God the mighty One) is my YESHUA (Jesus-in His pre-incarnation and eternal existence); I will trust and not be afraid:, for JAH-JAHOVAH is my strength and my song; He also is become my YESHUA (Jesus).... And the WORD (Jesus incarnate) became flesh, and dwelt among us. (John 1: 14). ... Therefore with joy shall ye draw water out of the wells of YESHUA [Jesus - waters of salvation flowing forth from Golgotha]."

Something very interesting occurred one spring in St. Louis: I was visiting in the home of our friends, Brother and Mrs. Charles Siegelman, and another Jew was present there. He claimed Jewish orthodoxy for his creed. Of course the conversation centered on Him Who is the Center of all things -- Jesus. This good Jewish brother opposed the claims of Yeshua in the Old Testament verbally, and in a friendly fashion, most violently. His best offensive weapon, he thought, was to fling at me and at all of us there the well-known challenge: "You can't find the name of 'Jesus' in the Old Testament;" and this he did.

I did not answer him directly, but asked him to translate for us from my Hebrew Bible, Isaiah 62:11. Being a Hebrew scholar, he did so with utmost ease, rapidly, and correctly; and here is what and how he translated that text verbatim: *"Behold, Jehovah has proclaimed unto the end of the world. Say ye to the daughter of Zion, Behold thy YESHUA [Jesus] cometh; behold, His reward is with Him, and His work before Him."* just then he crimsoned as he realized what he had done and how he had played into my hands, and he just fairly screamed out, "No! No! You made me read it 'thy YESHUA' Jesus], Mr. Glass! You tricked me!" I said, "No, I did not trick you, I just had you read the Word of God for yourself. Can't you see that here SALVATION is a Person and not a thing or an event? HE Comes, 'HIS reward is with HIM, and His work before him.' "Then he rushed at his own Old Testament, talking away frantically saying, "I'm sure mine is different from yours." And when he found the passage, he just dropped like a deflated balloon. His Old Testament was, of course, identical. All he could use as an escape from admitting defeat was to deny the divine inspiration of the book of Isaiah.

Then skipping on to Habakkuk, we have the greatest demonstration of the NAME "Jesus" in the Old Testament; for here we have both the name as well as the title of the Savior. In 3:13 we read literally from the original Hebrew:

"Thou wentest forth with the YESHA [variant of ESHUA-Jesus] of [or for] thy people; with YESHUA thy MESSIAH [thine Anointed

One: i.e., with Jesus thy Anointed] thou woundest the head of the house of the wicked one [Satan]."

Here you have it! The very NAME given to our Lord in the New Testament - JESUS CHRIST! So don't let anyone - Jew or Gentle - tell you that the Name JESUS is not found in the Old Testament. And so when the aged Simeon came to the Temple, led there by the Holy Spirit, and took the baby Yeshua in his arms, he said,

"Lord, now lettest thou thy servant depart in peace, according to thy word: For mine eyes have seen thy salvation [YESHUA (Jesus)]" (Luke 2:29-30).

Certainly! Not only did his eyes see God's Salvation - God's YESHUA (Jesus) - but he felt Him and touched Him. His believing heart beat with joy and assurance as he felt the loving heart of God throbbing in the heart of the holy infant YESHUA.

"And thou shalt call his name Jesus (SALVATION = YESHUA: for he shall save [salvage] his people from their sins!" ISAIAH 53

YESHUA IN ANCIENT HEBREW
Dr. Al Garza

When ancient Hebrew was first written, each letter represented both a sound and a picture. In Chinese and in ancient Egyptian every word is formed by adding pictures together to draw out the meaning of the word. This was also done in the ancient Hebrew; a word picture is a word that is described by pictures. Let us look at the entire Hebrew alphabet in the form of the pictograph script:

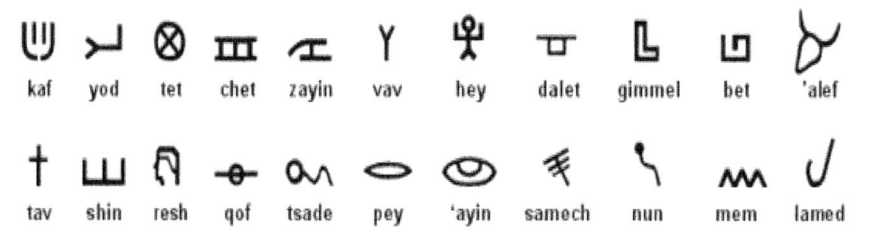

| kaf | yod | tet | chet | zayin | vav | hey | dalet | gimmel | bet | 'alef |

| tav | shin | resh | qof | tsade | pey | 'ayin | samech | nun | mem | lamed |

The entire Hebrew alphabet was written in picture form, from Alef to Tav[53]. The last letter and picture being the Tav is the picture of the cross. So if the Hebrews wanted to write a word using the pictures they would place them together and use the meaning of both pictures to communicate. For example, if they wanted to say *"father"* in Hebrew they would say "Ab". Now using the pictures they would put "Alef" and "Bet" together to say "Ab" or "father". Now let's look deeper into the meaning of the word *"father"* in Hebrew.

---

[53] Alef is Hebrew for ox while Tav is Hebrew for mark or sign also covenant.

Name	Pictograph	Meaning	Name	Pictograph	Meaning
Aleph		Ox / strength / leader	Lamed		Staff / goad / control / "toward"
Bet		House / "In"	Mem		Water / chaos
Gimmel		Foot / camel / pride	Nun		Seed / fish / activity / life
Dalet		Tent door / pathway	Samekh		Hand on staff / support / prop
Hey		Lo! Behold! "The"	Ayin		Eye / to see / experience
Vav		Nail / peg / add / "And"	Pey		Mouth / word / speak
Zayin		Plow / weapon / cut off	Tsade		Man on side / desire / need
Chet		Tent wall / fence / separation	Qof		Sun on horizon / behind
Tet		Basket / snake / surround	Resh		Head / person / first
Yod		Arm and hand / work / deed	Shin		Eat / consume / destroy
Kaf		Palm of hand / to open	Tav		Mark / sign / covenant

In the chart above you can see that the "Alef" is the picture of an ox or bull and the "Bet" is a picture of a house. The ox represents strength and leader while "Bet" represents a picture of a house. So together the word "Ab" means "father, leader of the house.", that is exactly what the scriptures teach about the father being the head of the house and the leader. Below you will see the chart for the word picture for both "father" and "God" and in Classical Hebrew.

"Word Picture"		Classical Hebrew	
Pictograph	Meaning	Hebrew	Meaning
	Strong Leader	אֵל	Name for God; "Strength." Used 250 times in the *Tanakh*.
	Strength (of the) house	אָב	Father

The name for "God" in Hebrew is "El" and as you can see above the word picture means *"God, the strong leader"*. This is how the ancient Hebrews wrote and communicated using word pictures. Now let us look at how the Hebrew language has evolved in Modern Hebrew.

Hebrew *(Ivrit:* עברית) is the name given to one of the world's oldest languages. The name derives from Eber *('ever)* the son of Shem; *'ever* means "region across or beyond" and derives from a root that means to pass over. Shem is called *"the father of all of the sons of Eber"* (Gen 10:21); and therefore Hebrew descendants are called Semites. In the Scriptures, Hebrew is used as an adjective (עברי) to describe Jews who are *"from the other side"* (i.e., of the Euphrates River). Modern Hebrew is called *Ivrit*.

In Bereshit[54] 31:47, Laban and Jacob refer to a heap of stones in their native speech. Laban uses the phrase "Yegar Sahaduta" which is Aramaic, but Jacob uses *"Gal-Ed"* which is Hebrew. The Garden of Eden, or *gan eden* is known as the first paradise, the location for the origin of man made *b'tzelem elohim,* in the image of God. This image included the ability to use a God-given language (a theory that an original source language was given in Eden is called "Edenics"). Man was exiled from Eden, however, and began to be dispersed upon the face of the earth. The Great Flood, or *mabul* effected judgment upon the antediluvian clans for their constant wickedness

---

[54] Bereshit is Hebrew for the Greek Genesis

before YHWH, the only survivors were the direct descendants of the clan of Noach. The Toldot b'nei Noach (the generations of Noah, or Table of 70 Nations as listed in Genesis 10) indicates some of the earliest migration of clans. Noah's son Shem is also called *"the father of all of the sons of Eber"* (Gen 10:21); his toldot is given in Genesis 11:10. The Tower of Babel, or *migdal bavel* located in the *"plains of Shinar"* of ancient Mesopotamia (Gen 11:1-9) is historically identified as the original site of ancient Babylon. Perhaps the tower was a form of idolatrous ziggurat meant to unify the ancients.

Abraham, a descendant of the clan of Eber, was called by God from Ur of the Chaldees (i.e., *kasdim*) in 1800 BCE to the land of Canaan. The language in Canaan at that time has been called "proto-Canaanite," the parent language of the dialects of Hittites, Amorites, Hivites, Jebusites, Perizites. In relation to the Hebrews, proto-Canaanite script may be called *ketav Ivri*.

During the 400 years that Abraham's clan was in Egypt (Genesis 15:13), the Hebrews still spoke a Canaanite variant (e.g. Yoseph's brothers in Egypt: see Genesis 42:23). An article of orthodox Jewish faith is that God originally revealed the Torah to Mosheh using *Ketav Ashurit* (from *ashrei*), not *ketav Ivri,* since the earlier script was considered profane and riddled with paganism. After Mosheh broke the first set of tablets, however, God wrote the second set using the profane script. After the Babylonian captivity, ketav Ashurit was fully restored to the Jewish people by Ezra the Scribe and came to be called *Lashon HaKodesh* (the holy language). This same script has been used until this day for the writing of Torah scrolls. Modern soferut (scribal arts) include the Bet Yosef, Bet Ari, and Sephard styles of ketav Ashurit for Sifrei Torah (torah scrolls). A Midrash on the *Migdal Bavel* (Tower of Babel) teaches that at the end of time all people will once again speak one language and that will be a purified form of the Hebrew tongue. There is also d'rash on the verse: *"For then I will make the peoples pure of speech, so that they all invoke YHWH by name and serve Him with one accord"* (Zeph 3:9) that indicates the same. The Hebrew from the beginning, as we will see below, has changed dramatically.

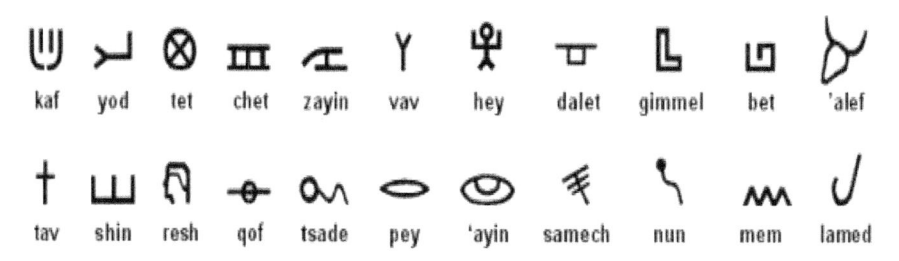

kaf	yod	tet	chet	zayin	vav	hey	dalet	gimmel	bet	'alef

tav	shin	resh	qof	tsade	pey	'ayin	samech	nun	mem	lamed

Proto-Canaanite Pictographs

ḥēt / ḥ	zayin / z	wāw / w	hē / h	dālet / d	gīmel / g	bēt / b	'ālef / '
sāmek / s	nun / n	mēm / m	lāmed / l	kaf / k	yōd / y	ṭēt / ṭ	
tāw / t	śin/šin / š	rēš / r	qōf / q	ṣādē / ṣ	pē / p	'ayin / '	

The Phoenician Script

kaf	yod	tet	het	zayin	waw	he	dalet	gimel	beyt	'alef
k	y	t	h	z	w	h	d	g	b	'

taw	šin	reš	qop	sade	pe	'ayin	samek	nun	mem	lamed
t	š	r	q	ṣ	p	'	s	n	m	l

Proto Hebrew Script

kaf	yod	tet	chet	zayin	vav	he	dalet	gimel	bet	alef
k	y	t	h	z	w	h	d	g	b	'

tav	shin	resh	kof	tzadi	pe	ayin	samech	nun	mem	lamed
t	sh	r	k	tz	p	'	s	n	m	l

The Samaritan Script

כ/ך	י	ט	ח	ז	ו	ה	ד	ג	ב	א
kaf	yod	tet	chet	zayin	vav	hey	dalet	gimmel	bet	'alef

ת	ש/שׂ	ר	ק	צ/ץ	פ/ף	ע	ס	נ/ן	מ/ם	ל
tav	shin	resh	qof	tsade	pey	'ayin	samech	nun	mem	lamed

Classical Hebrew Script

ק	י	८	ח	ל	ו	ה	?	८	ב	k
kaf	yod	tet	chet	zayin	vav	he	dalet	gimel	bet	alef

ת	ل	ר	p	צ 3	פ ס	ү	o	נ	מ	ל
tav	shin/sin	resh	kof	tzadi(k)	pe	ayin	samech	nun	mem	lamed

Modern Hebrew Cursive

כ ך	י	ט	ח	ז	ו	ה	ד	ג	ב	א
kaf	yod	tet	chet	zayin	vav	he	dalet	gimel	bet	alef

ת	ש	ר	ק	צ ץ	פ ף	ע	ס	נ ן	מ ם	ל
tav	shin/sin	resh	kof	tzadi(k)	pe	ayin	samech	nun	mem	lamed

Rashi-Style Hebrew

The **Rashi style** is used mainly to write commentaries on texts. It is named in honor of Rabbi Shlomo Yitzchaki (1040-1105 AD) a.k.a. Rashi, one of the greatest medieval Jewish scholars and bible commentators.

There are some scholars who divide the Hebrew language into four basic periods.

1. **Biblical Hebrew** – aka Classical Hebrew; by the time of Jesus, Aramaic was the common language, but Hebrew was used in synagogues and in Temple worship. Jesus knew and spoke Biblical Hebrew.

2. **Mishnaic Hebrew** – aka Rabbinic Hebrew; Talmud and Midrash; 2nd century AD. Note that the grammar and vocabulary of this Hebrew is very different than Biblical Hebrew.
3. **Medieval Hebrew** – Used to translate Arabic works into Hebrew, e.g., Maimonides and other medievalists.
4. **Modern Hebrew** – 19th century to present. Eliezar Ben Yehuda (1858-1922) led the rebirth of Hebrew as a spoken language. After immigrating to Israel in 1881, he began promoting the use of Hebrew at home and in the schools.

Scholars are uncertain how far back ketav Ivri goes in Jewish history, though it appears to date to at least the 10th century BC. The work of some paleolinguists suggests that an even earlier form of Canaanite cuneiform is actually the basis of ketav Ivri. These **Hebrew Word Pictures** are regarded as the most ancient form of Hebrew known. Here is a simplified illustration of the progression of the script forms (left-to-right, oldest to newest):

The Aleph and the Taw

The Messiah Jesus said that He is the *Aleph* and the *Tav*, the First *(rishon)* and the Last *(acharon)*, and the Beginning *(rosh)* and the Ending *(sof)*

אני האלף והתו הראש והסוף הראשון והאחרון:

"I am the 'Aleph' and the 'Taw', the Beginning and the End, the First and the Last."[55]

When Yeshua said this, he was making a direct reference to Isaiah 41:4, 44:6, and 48:12, where YHWH Himself says that He is the First and the Last -- and explicitly declared that there is no other Elohim beside Him.

Please get a hold of the implication here: Yeshua of Nazareth was claiming that He was the one to whom the references in Isaiah pertain. He is the *"direct object"* of which the Scriptures speak.

Jesus also said He was the Truth of God Himself:

אָנֹכִי הַדֶּרֶךְ וְהָאֱמֶת וְהַחַיִּים
וְאִישׁ לֹא־יָבֹא אֶל־הָאָב בִּלְתִּי עַל־יָדִי

---

[55] The Scriptures Bible 1988

"I am the way and the truth and the life; no man comes to the Father apart from me"[56] (John 14:6)

Notice that the word for truth (*emet*) contains the first letter *aleph* the middle letter *mem* and the last letter *taw* of the Hebrew alphabet, which the Jewish sages say means that the truth contains everything from Aleph to Taw:

אֱמֶת

28	27	26	25	24	23	22	21	20	19	18	17	16	15	14	13	12	11	10	9	8	7	6	5	4	3	2	1
ת	שׁ	שׂ	ר	ק	צ	ף	פ	ע	ס	ן	נ	ם	מ	ל	ך	כ	י	ט	ח	ז	ו	ה	ד	ג	ב	א

What is Truth?

The Hebrew word *emet* has a more concrete meaning than the English word for *"truth"* (the English word derives from the Greek/Western view of truth as a form of correspondence between language and reality, but invariably languished over epistemological questions that led, ultimately, to skepticism). In the Hebraic mindset, the person who acts in *emet* is one who can be *trusted* (Gen. 24:49; 42:16; 47:26; Josh. 2:14). Actions, speech, reports, or judgment are *emet* because they are *reliable* (Dt. 13:14; 22:20; 1 Kg. 10:6; 22:16; Pr. 12:19; Zech. 8:16). If a seed is a seed of *emet*, its quality is *trustworthy* (Jer. 2:21).

---

[56] Yohanan 14:6

In the Tanakh, *emet* is often coupled with *chesed,* covenant faithfulness, which designates Elohim loyalty in fulfilling his promises and his covenant. For example, Elohim *emet* and *chesed* were majestically revealed in giving the covenant at Sinai (Ex. 34:6).

יְהוָה יְהוָה אֵל רַחוּם וְחַנּוּן אֶרֶךְ אַפַּיִם וְרַב־חֶסֶד וֶאֱמֶת

YHWH, YHWH, El, merciful and gracious, longsuffering, and abundant in goodness and truth (Exodus 34:6).

Indeed, Pilate's question, *"What is truth?"* is a category mistake, since truth is not about "what" but about "Who." That is, truth is not something objective and static, a thing to be known and studied from a distance. No. Truth is essentially personal. It is personal disclosure of the character of the subject. Understood in this way, truth is a way of living, a mode of existence, a relational truth.

הוּא אוֹר אֱמֶת אֲשֶׁר בָּא לָעוֹלָם לְהָאִיר לְכָל־אָדָם

"He is the true Light, who lights every man that comes into the world"[57] (John 1:9).

---

[57] *Hu or emet asher ba la'olam l'ha'ir l'khol-adam* Hebrew transliteration.

Yeshua is the Direct Object

Interestingly, Aleph and Tav form a unique word that functions as a *"direct object marker"* in the both Biblical and modern Hebrew:

את

As it is written in Genesis 1:1, *"In the beginning Elohim (ALEPH/TAV) created the heavens and the earth."*[58]

בְּרֵאשִׁית בָּרָא אֱלֹהִים אֵת הַשָּׁמַיִם וְאֵת הָאָרֶץ

Considered this way, Yeshua is the Direct Object of the Universe, the End *(sof)* of all of creation. And not only is Yeshua the End of all creation, but He is the *"Beginning of the Creation of Elohim,"* the Creator and Sustainer of all things:

"For by him were all things created that are in heaven, and that are in earth, visible and invisible, whether they be thrones, or dominions, or principalities, or powers: all things were created by him and for him: And he is before all things and by him all things consist." (Colossians 1:16-17)

---

[58] Bereshit 1:1 "Barashit bara Elohim et Hashamayim het haaretz"

כֹּה אָמַר הָאָמֵן עֵד הָאֱמֶת וְהַצֶּדֶק וְרֵאשִׁית בְּרִיאַת הָאֱלֹהִים

"Thus says the Amen, the faithful and true witness, the beginning of the creation of God" [59] (Rev. 3:14).

Yeshua is the Strong Sign

Finally, using the ancient **pictographs**, we can see that Yeshua is the *"Strong Sign and Covenant"* from YHWH:

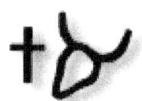

†𐤀

He is the One who comes in humble, silent strength (Aleph) bearing the Sign of the true Covenant of God (Tav).

The Taw

What we have learned so far is that the ancient Hebrew alphabet is not the same as the Modern Hebrew alphabet. The original Hebrew letters were all pictures used to form words. The question now is what role did the Hebrew letter pictures play in regards to Yeshua? We must first understand that just like the prophecies concerning the Messiah in the Tanakh (Old Testament) did not literally say this was about Yeshua (Jesus), the Hebrew picture letters do not literally say that this is about Yeshua either. What they do reveal, just like the

---

[59] *Ko amar ha'amein 'ed ha'emet v'hatsedek v'reishit b'riat ha'elohim*

Tanakh prophecies of the Messiah, is a clearer understanding of the sacrifice and redemptive plan of Yeshua after the fact. When the ancient Taw cross is combined with other picture letters in the ancient Hebrew alphabet something revealing is discovered. The veil is moved to see and understand that YHWH God had put his redemptive plan in the very language he created for his Jewish people. YHWH has preserved his language and in it He has preserved the testimony of the work of Yeshua the Jewish Messiah and his role from the foundation of the world. When Yeshua died on the cross, he died on the ancient Hebrew symbol for covenant. The combining form of the Hebrew picture letters with the Taw cross is just the beginning.

There are times when the letter or word has a clear message for us. This is the case with the last letter of the Hebrew alphabet. Taw which literally means the *"sign of the covenant or mark of the covenant"* is spelled in Modern Hebrew תו. The first letter that is used to spell out Taw in Hebrew is the picture of the cross while the second letter in the word, **waw** or **vav** in Modern Hebrew, is the picture of a nail.[60]

Y   +

Waw   Taw

When we look at the fact that the very word for sign, covenant and

---

[60] The Hebrew picture for the Hebrew word "taw" is the cross and the nail when read from right to left in Hebrew.

mark in Hebrew it is a picture of a cross and a nail. This carries a powerful prophetic significance. We can now better understand the Apostle Sha'ul (Paul) in his letter to the Qolasim (Colossians) when he says,

"having blotted out the handwriting of ordinances that was against us, which was contrary to us, and He has taken it out of the way, ***nailing*** *it to* ***the cross.****"* [61]

This is a clear reference to the very word of the Taw which is spelled out in ancient Hebrew with the picture of a cross and a nail. Shall we believe that this is all a coincidence or that the Elohim of Israel preserved, within the ancient Hebrew language, the true redemptive plan of salvation through the Messiah Yeshua?

Now let us look at the Hebrew word Torah. There is no word more Jewish than the word Torah. The word Torah means *"teaching"* in Hebrew.

Hey   Resh   Waw   Taw

The meaning of this word can be found in the letters that form the Hebrew word that means *teaching*. When the Hebrew letter ***"Hey"*** is placed as the last letter of the word, it means *"what is revealed*

---

[61] Colossians 2:14 in the Hebrew Sod level of interpretation.

from"[62]. Now look at the first three Hebrew letters and what do they tell us the teaching comes from? The Hebrew letter **"resh"** means *"the man or head"* (second to last letter of *hey*) and the next letter is **"waw"** or **"vav"** and it means *"nail"* and the last Hebrew letter is of course the **"taw"** or the cross (the picture to the far right). So now we can see the true meaning behind the word Torah,

"The teaching is revealed from the man nailed to the cross."

*"For **Torah** shall go forth from Zion, and the word of YHWH from Jerusalem."* [63]

Yeshua himself made this statement in Mattithyahu 5:17 (Matthew), *"Think not that I came to destroy the **Torah** or the prophets: I came not to destroy, but to fulfill."* Yeshua was going to fulfill what the Torah and the prophets had spoken about concerning him. What was revealed from the Torah was Yeshua death on the cross. The ancient Hebrew word picture for Torah reveals this. This is no coincidence that Yeshua died on the cross and within the ancient Hebrew language we can find such meaning concerning his death. The Torah has revealed the man nailed to the cross.

Another Hebrew word to look at is the word Sabbath or Sha-bat in Hebrew. The meaning of this word is of course is *"rest"* but the

---

[62] Hebrew is always read from right to left

[63] Micah 4:2

Hebrew word picture tells us something deeper. The word Sha-bat uses the Hebrew letters Shin, Bet and Taw and together they form the Hebrew Sha-bat or Sabbath. If you take away the last Hebrew letter, the Taw, you have the Hebrew word "Shoov" which means *"repent and return to."* But repent and return to what? The cross of course! The Taw cross at the end of the word reveals the true meaning of the word Sha-bat. It literally means, *"Repent and return to the cross for rest."* Looking back at Shemoth (Exodus) 20:8 in the Tanakh we can see a whole new meaning to the passage.

*"Remember the **Sha-bat** day, to keep it holy…"*[64]

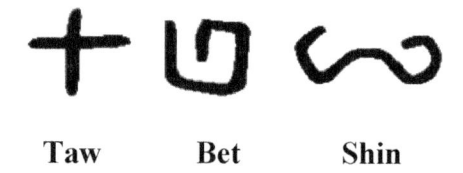

Taw   Bet   Shin

There are those who don't understand the meaning behind the word Sha-bat and have turned it into a religious ritual. In times we need to look a little deeper[65] into a word root to get the full effect of what it means. Some words are combined word forms that have meaning when they are divided into their original form. In this case the first two letters, Shin and Bet, together mean *"repent and return too"* while the last letter, Taw, means *"covenant"* or just the cross.

---

[64] Exodus 20:8

[65] The level Sod in Hebrew means hidden or secret

In the Brit Hadasha[66] scriptures there are many references to the cross and its true meaning once we understand its ancient use in the Hebrew language. In other times the word simply is in reference to one's own sacrifice in order to follow Yeshua. It is after the death, burial and resurrection of Yeshua that we see the impact of the word. When Yeshua was hanging on the cross he said *"It is finished!"* What was finished? Now that we understand that the Taw cross means covenant, sign and mark we can see the impact of Yeshua words. The fulfillment of the final covenant by Yeshua death on the Taw cross was the predetermine plan of YHWH from the beginning foretold in the ancient Hebrew letter pictures. Yeshua himself said,

*"This cup which is poured out for you is the **new covenant** in My blood."* Luqas (Luke) 22:20.

Even Sha'ul knew the importance of the Taw cross when he said,

*"…and might reconcile them both in one body to Elohim through the **cross, by it** having put to death the enmity."* Eph'siyim (Ephesians) 2:16.

Then again he says, *"… and through Him to reconcile all things to Himself, having made peace through the blood of **His cross**; through Him, I say, whether things on earth or things in heaven."* Qolasim[67]

---

[66] New Testament or New Covenant

[67] The Hebrew word for the Greek Colossians

(Colossians 1:20)

The final redemptive plan of God was fulfilled on the Taw cross.

The Message
*"For **the message of the cross** is to them that perish foolishness; but unto us who are saved it is the power of God."* Sha'ul in Qorintiyim Aleph 1:18 (1 Corinthians 1:18)

In the conclusion of the ancient Hebrew Taw cross we must summarize the message it foretells concerning Yeshua and the redemptive plan of salvation by the fulfillment of the covenant made by YHWH to his people and the world. Let's begin with the Hebrew word *"redeem"* which in Hebrew is ga'el and looks like this:

Lamed   Aleph   Gamel

The Hebrew letter Gamel[68] means to *"lift up"* and the next two letters together spell out El (God in singular form). The word picture for *"redeem"* is *"when God is lifted up"*. This takes us right back to Yeshua when he said,

"And I, if I am lifted up from the land, will draw all men to Myself...The Son of Man must be lifted up."

---

[68] The letter or picture Gamel is to the right in Hebrew.

These versus spoken by Yeshua in Yohanan[69] 12:32-34 foretell His death in which we are redeemed by His death on the Taw cross. In the language of the Jews, to be lifted up was an expression of being put to death. We see this in verse 34 when the crowd responded to Him. Redemption comes when El (God) is lifted up and since Yeshua is El and came to redeem man by sacrificing Himself for us, we can see how the word picture for *"redeem"* tells this story. Sha'ul[70] when writing to Titos (Titus) said,

*"...who gave himself for us, that he might **redeem** (ga'El) us from all iniquity, and purify unto himself a people for his own possession, zealous of good works."*[71]

So we are redeemed because El was lifted up unto death for us so that we could be saved.

When we consider how El rescued his people out of Egypt we can't forget when he told his people to put a sign on the door in blood so death would pass over them. Today this memorial is celebrated by the Jews and it is called The Passover. It is an everlasting Torah from generation to generation. Let's take a closer look at the word used for *"sign"* in ancient Hebrew and see what the word picture tells us. In Shemoth (Exodus) 12:13 we read the following,

---

[69] John 12:32-34

[70] Paul the disciple of Yeshua.

[71] Titus 2:14

*"The blood shall be a **sign** for you on the houses where you live; and when I see the blood I will pass over you, and no plague will befall you to destroy you when I strike the land of Egypt."*

The Hebrew word for *sign* or *seal* is *"oht"* and begins with *aleph* then *waw* and finally the *taw*. So what does the sign or seal tell us in the Hebrew word pictures? *"The Leader Nailed to the Cross."*

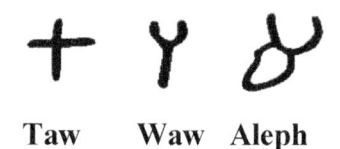

Taw   Waw   Aleph

Remember that *Aleph*[72] means *Leader* and *Waw* means *Nail* and of course *taw* means *Cross*. This is the true word picture meaning of The Passover. As the Hebrews were delivered from death by putting the blood of the lamb over the doorposts, so the blood of Yeshua the true Lamb of Elohim delivers and redeems us from eternal death by His death on the cross. The blood was a sign or a seal for the Hebrews and it is our sign and seal for us today.

We now need to look at the Hebrew word for "Son" and "Covenant". The word *son* in Hebrew is *Bar* in and if you add the Hebrew letter *Yod* to the end it will now become the Hebrew word for *"My Son"* or *"The Son of."* See below for the word picture.

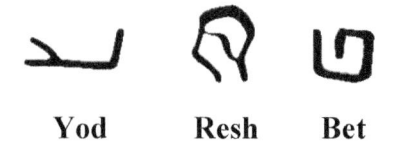

Yod   Resh   Bet

---

[72] Aleph in Hebrew means ox and represents strength and leader.

With that in mind we can now add the next Hebrew letter *taw* to the end next to the *yod* and we will make the Hebrew word Covenant (Barit). See below for the complete ancient word picture script.

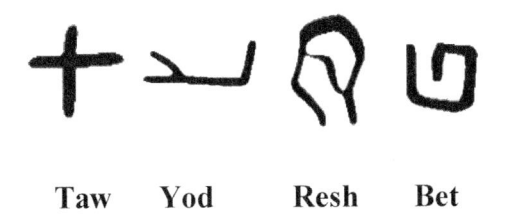

Taw　Yod　　Resh　　Bet

If I add one more letter to the beginning of this word[73] we can spell another Hebrew word. If I place the Hebrew letter *ayin*[74] in front of the *bet* we would make the word for *Hebrew* (Evrit).

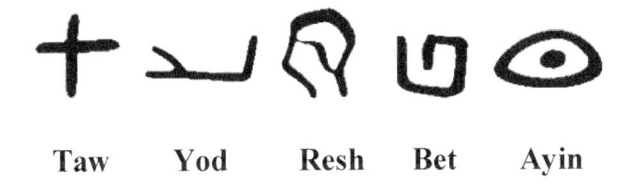

Taw　Yod　　Resh　　Bet　　Ayin

So what does the word picture for *Hebrew* tell us? It says, *"See the Hebrew covenant of the son on the cross"* or *"The Hebrew covenant is the Son on the Cross."* This ancient Hebrew word picture for *Hebrew* reveals YHWH son on the cross as the true and final covenant to man which Yeshua had to fulfill. These ancient Hebrew word pictures don't contradict what has already taken place, but only strengthens the message of Yeshua and the redemptive work on the cross.

---

[73] The beginning of this word starts to the right with Bet.

[74] The Hebrew letter Ayin means eye or see in the picture form.

Elohim sent the eternal Word[75] to become a perfect man in the body of Yeshua to fulfill what the Torah and the prophets had written concerning him,

"They pierced my hands and my feet...and they shall look upon me (YHWH Yeshua) *whom they have pierce."* Tehillim 22:16 (Psalms) and Zekaryah 12:10 (Zechariah) Yeshua himself in Luqas (Luke) 24:25-27 said, *"And He said to them, O foolish ones, and slow of heart to believe on all things which the prophets spoke! Was it not necessary for the Christ to suffer these things, and to enter into His glory? And beginning from Mosheh, and from all the prophets, He explained to them the things about Himself in all the Scriptures."*

The final ancient Hebrew word picture that I would like to look at is the very covenant name of Elohim. The very name revealed to Mosheh and the Hebrew people that would be for eternity. The name Yahweh or YHWH, without the vowels, is the most sacred name in all of scripture. Modern Jews will not even attempt to pronounce the name in fear of blasphemy. In some of the earliest writings found in the Dead Sea scrolls we find written in them the very name of YHWH. In this passage in Psalms 119:56-64 we see the name.

---

[75] John 1:1

When we go back further to the ancient word picture of the name of God we see this:

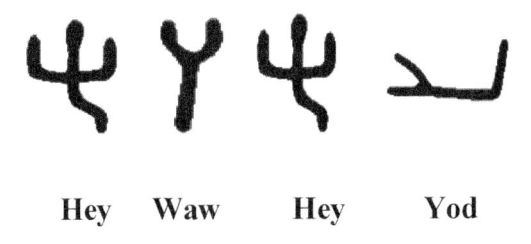

Hey   Waw   Hey   Yod

What does this ancient word picture of the name of Elohim tell us? The first Hebrew letter is the *yod* and means *"hand"* while the second and last Hebrew letter is the *hey* and is a picture of a man with his hands upward. This has the meaning also of *"lo behold or look"* The *waw* in the middle is of course the *"nail"* There are several possibilities for a word picture. One could be, *"Behold and look at the Nail in my Hand"*, or *"Look at the nail and Behold my Hand"* or again, *"Behold the Nail in my Hand"* This should remind us of what Yeshua said to his disciples after his resurrection.

"See My hands and My feet, that it is I Myself."[76]

No matter how you connect the word picture, one thing is clear, the message is there. Not everyone will agree with the things shown in this book but we cannot just dismiss them without examining them. Even if you refuse to accept anything written, that will not change the fact that there lived a man name Yeshua (Jesus) who claimed to

---
[76] Luke 24:39

be the Jewish Messiah, YHWH Elohim, and who gave and sacrificed himself on the *cross* for what the scriptures call the sins of the world.

The Taw: Jewish and Christian Scholars

As we talk about the cross we must understand that there is a Hebrew word for cross that is used today in Modern Hebrew. The Hebrew word for cross is ts'lav (צלב) and once you understand that the Jews believed that the sign of YHWH in Yehezqel 9 was in the form of the ancient Taw cross then the Hebrew word picture seen in ts'lav makes sense. The Taw cross was Elohim sign for the righteous of heart who did not follow after the wicked rulers of Israel. The first letter used in ts'lav is the Hebrew Tsadik which means a *righteous man.* The modern shape of the letter is said to represent a person on their knees with their hands raised to Elohim. The next two letters spell the word *lev*, which means *a heart.* We can see that the Hebrew word used to describe the cross, the shape of the ancient Taw, is described in the Hebrew word picture as *The Righteous Heart.* The above ts'lav is spelled out from right to left in Hebrew. So we can see it is through the righteous heart of Yeshua (Jesus) that he confirmed the strong covenant of YHWH by dying on the Taw cross.

In the New Dictionary by Avraham Eben-Shoshan, who has written one of the most authoritative resources in Israel, he comments on the ancient Canaanite-Hebrew Alef-Bet usage of the final letter Tav. Next is a copy of the comment and is translated in Dr. Frank T. Seekins booklet, The Ancient Tav.

> *Translated it says...*
>
> תי״ו, תו ‭,‬ שֵׁם הָאוֹת הָאַחֲרוֹנָה בָּאָלֶף־בֵּית הָעִבְרִי, ת
> [על שם צורתה הקדומה ✗ או ✗ ‭,‬ וְסִימָן
> בָּאָלֶף־בֵּית הַכְּנַעֲנִי־הָעִבְרִי הַקַּדְמוֹן].
>
> Tav, The name of the final letter in the Hebrew Alef-Bet, ת [for the ancient ✗ or ✗, A sign of marking, in the ancient Canaanite-Hebrew Alef-Bet.

Avraham Rosenstein, later Avraham Eben-Shoshan was born in 1946-1958. Eben-Shoshan compiled *HaMilon HeHadash* (New Dictionary of the Hebrew Language), which became known as the Eben-Shoshan Dictionary. The completed dictionary consisted of 24,698 main entries. He was also the author of the Eben-Shoshan concordance and co-author of the Bialik concordance.

In the Gesenius Hebrew-Chaldee Lexicon to the Old Testament we have also a reference to the Taw or Tav. Gesenius explains that in Yehezqel 9:4 (Ezekiel) *a sign*, was in the form of a cross and the coins of the Maccabees had the form of the cross on them.

*See copy of lexicon on the next page.

> תָו m. (for תָוֶה), from the root תָוָה No. 1) -
> (1) *a sign*, Eze. 9:4. (Arab. وَسْم، سِمَة a sign in the form of a cross branded on the thigh or neck of horses or camels, whence the name of the letter ת, which in Phoenician, and on the coins of the Maccabees has the form of a cross. From the Phoenicians the Greeks and the Romans took both the name and form of the letter.)
>
> (2) *sign* (cruciform), *mark* subscribed instead of a name to a bill of complaint; hence *subscription*, Job 31:35. It is state that at the Synod of Chalcedon and other synods principally in the East, some even of the bishops being unable to write, put the sign of the cross instead of their names, which is still often done by common people in legal proceedings; so that in the infancy of the art of writing this could not fail of being the case, so as for the expression to be received into the usage of language.

Heinrich Friedrich Wilhelm Gesenius (3 February 1786 – 23 October 1842) was a German orientalist and Biblical critic. As an exegete he exercised a powerful influence on theological investigation.

Looking also into the different translations of the Bible we can see in their footnotes and commentaries their understanding of the ancient Hebrew letter Taw. Their understanding gives insight into the usage of the ancient letter and how it was known in its original form.
The Douay Rheims version taken from the Vulgate in 1749-1752

shows the same understanding of Taw as Thau or the ancient Hebrew letter shaped like a cross. In Douay Rheims footnote on Yehezqel 9 he states, *"Mark Thau, or Tau, is the last letter in the Hebrew alphabet, and signifies a sign, or a mark; which is the reason why some translators render this place set a mark, or mark a mark, without specifying what this mark was. But St. Jerome, and other interpreters, conclude it was in the form of the letter Thau."*[77] The Douay Rheims footnote concludes the clear understanding and meaning of the ancient Taw cross from the Greek Thau. He references Jerome and other interpreters as having this knowledge as well. The Greek letter Thau was in the shape of a cross like image.

James Martin was a translator for The Commentary of the Old Testament by C.F. Keil and F. Delitzsch. This work is a foundational Protestant commentary. In it we find on Yehezqel 9:4 the following, *"And Jehovah said to him, Go through the midst of the city, through the midst of Jerusalem, and mark a **cross** upon the foreheads of the men who sigh and groan over all the abominations which take place in their midst..."*[78] This foundational commentary clearly uses the cross in its translation of Yehezqel 9:4. The ancient Hebrew letter Taw was still understood to be a cross.

In the New American Bible on this same passage of Yehezqel 9:4 they translate the verse as the following, *"saying to him: Pass*

---

[77] The Douay Rheims version taken from the Vulgate in 1749-1752

[78] Commentary of the Old Testament by C.F. Keil and F. Delitzsch.

*through the city (through Jerusalem) and mark an **X** on the foreheads of those who moan and groan over all the abominations that are practiced within it."* The New American Bible then goes on the comment by saying, "An X: literally the Hebrew letter *taw*, which had the form of a cross." To mark an X was to put the letter Taw on the forehead which was the cross. Translation after translation we continue to see the clear understanding of the ancient Hebrew letter Taw. There is no mistaking such a usage of the Taw cross in the Tanakh.

Other Bible translations such as the Darby Bible and the French Jerusalem Bible have the same usage of the Taw cross in Yehezqel 9:4. In the French Jerusalem Bible it says, "a mark of the cross" in French, (et marquee d'une croix). John Darby who was a leader of the Plymouth Brethren and who is considered the father of modern Dispensationalism said, "Tau, the name of the last letter of the Hebrew alphabet." Jewish, Catholic and Protestant scholars have taught the ancient Jewish teaching of the Hebrew letter Taw as the shape of the cross and the sign of God on the forehead in Yehezqel 9:4.

This picture of the ancient Taw below was carved in stone about 3800 years ago (300 years before Mosheh aka Moses) at Wadi Al Hol, Egypt.

The cross of our Messiah has been revealed over a thousand years before Yeshua. It speaks of Elohim word, love and protection.

A FORMER RABBI SPEAKS

Born in Germany, of orthodox Jewish parents, my first fifteen years were saturated with training in Orthodox Judaism. Then I began my studies toward a career, and was apprenticed to a manufacturer, doing office work. Although I continued to read the prayers and attend synagogue, my worldly associates led me into sinful pleasures and I drifted from the faith of my fathers.

My parents sent me to America to study in the Hebrew Union College in Ohio. There were major adjustments to be made, but I finished my training in all phases of Hebrew learning, completed my undergraduate work and received, eventually, my Master's degree. Having become proficient in translation of Hebrew into the vernacular, and with a complete knowledge of Jewish history, I was ordained and inducted into the rabbinical office. In my first charge I served ten years, receiving many tokens of affection from my flock. I contributed much to their knowledge of the social, industrial, and economic problems of the day. I spoke on monotheism, ethical culture, and the moral systems of the Jews. On Sabbath mornings I gave addresses on the Pentateuch and on Sundays I taught from eight in the morning to five in the evening with only one hour's break for dinner.

I became popular as a public speaker and was often asked to speak in Christian churches. Well do I recall the day when I proudly stood before an audience of professing Christians and told them why I was a Jew and would not believe in their Christ as my Messiah Savior. I gloried in the Reform Judaism that acknowledges no need of an atoning sacrifice for sin, a religion of ethics which quieted qualms of conscience through a smug self-righteousness. In that audience sat a humble, elderly woman who prayed, "O God, bring Dr. Wertheimer to realize his utter need of that Savior he so boastingly rejects! Bring him, if necessary, to the very depths in order that he may know his need of my Lord Jesus Christ."

What did I need of Jesus? I was perfectly satisfied with life. My wife was young, attractive and accomplished. I was rabbi of the B'nai Yeshorum Synagogue, lived in a beautiful home, and enjoyed a place of prominence in the community where I spoke in every denominational church, was honorary member of the Ministerial Association, served as Chaplain in the Masonic Lodge, and faired sumptuously every day.

Suddenly there came a change. My wife became seriously ill and was soon dead, leaving me a distraught widower with two small children. I could not sleep; I walked the streets striving to find something that would make me forget the void in my life. My dreams were shattered. Where was comfort to be found? I called on the God of my fathers, but the heavens seemed as brass. How could I speak words of comfort to others when my own sorrow had brought me to despair? I delved into Spiritism, Theosophy and Christian Science only to find them futile and hopeless.

I decided that I must resign and take time to think things through. I was perplexed about one thing in particular. Where was the spirit and soul of my loved one who had made my existence so sweet? What had become of her faculties and the intents and purposes of that active, keen mind? I turned to the Bible for an answer.

Again I studied Judaism, but it answered no questions, it satisfied no craving in my heart. Then I began to read the New Testament, comparing it with the Old. In the fifty-third chapter of Isaiah I was perplexed by the expression, '...my righteous servant?' I found he was going to beer the iniquity of Israel. I decided it could not mean Israel, for the prophet spoke of them as a sinful nation, laden with iniquity. Who was it?

I began to study the context and in Isaiah 50:6 I found, *"I gave My back to the smiters."* Then I read how the chapter began: *"Thus said Jehovah."* I asked, does God have a back? Did He give it to the smiters? Then I read he *"gave his checks to them that pluck off the hair."* And how he hid not His face *"from shame and spitting."* I asked myself, when did Jehovah have these human characteristics? When and why did He suffer these indignities? I was further perplexed by Psalm 110:1.

In my confusion I began to read Isaiah from the beginning. I was stopped at the sixth verse of chapter nine: *"For unto us a child is born, unto us a son is given, and the government shall be upon His shoulders: His name shall be called Wonderful, Counselor, The*

Mighty God, The Everlasting Father, The Prince of Peace." Here was a most incomprehensible thing!

I was suddenly faced with the doctrine of the Trinity. What now about our popular monotheistic slogan, "Sh'ma Isroel, Adonai Eloheynu, Adonai, Echod." Upon that word "Echod" (one) the entire philosophy of Judaism is based. I had been taught by the rabbis that echod means absolute unity. I began to study that word and found to my amazement it was used of Adam and Eve, who became one. It was used again when the spies returned from Canaan with a cluster of grapes (Eshol Echod). It was used again when the "men of Judah" stood up as one man" (Ish Echod). Suddenly I was struck with the error I had believed and proclaimed all through my ministry. Echod cannot mean absolute unity, but a composite unity.

Next I began to search for the name of Jesus in the Old Testament. In my study I found that 275 years before Christ, King Ptolemy Philadelphus summoned men from Palestine and commanded them to translate the Hebrew Scriptures into the Greek vernacular. "They took the Pentateuch first, and when they came to "Joshua" they translated it the book of "Jesous," written with a circumflex over it, to show that there had been a suppression of the Hebrew that could not be expressed in Greek. When Joshua went into Canaan with the other eleven spies, he was called "Yehoshuah" (Jehovah is Savior). That is exactly what the word "Jesus" means.

I could hold out in unbelief no longer. I was convinced of the truth of God as it is in Christ Jesus. I cried, "Lord, I believe that Thou as Jehovah Yesous has made atonement for me. I believe that Jehova Yesous died for me. I believe that Thou have made provision for me. From henceforth I will publicly confess Yeshuah as my Saviour and Lord." *Thus, after months of searching, I was convinced that Jesus was the righteous servant of Jehovah, (Jehovah-tsidkenu), "The Lord our righteousness."*

While I had served as a rabbi I had yearned to give the bereaved some hope and comfort, but I could not give what I did not possess. Now I could approach those in heartbreaking grief and tragedy and give them the satisfying words of the Lord Jesus,

"I am the resurrection and the life; he that believeth in Me, though he were dead, yet shall he live; and whosoever liveth and believed in Me shall never die." And again, *"Verily, verily I say unto you: He that heareth My Word, and believeth on Him that sent Me, hath (possesses now) everlasting life, and shall not come into condemnation, but is passed from death unto life."*

"There is but one eternal life, and one source of eternal life; that is God's Son. What a great and glorious message we, His redeemed ones, are commissioned to deliver today."

*Personal Testimony of Dr. Max Wertheimer, a former Rabbi of Temple Israel in Dayton Ohio.

REFERENCES

1 The Tenach is a short hand reference for the Holy Scriptures, consisting of the Books of Moses. the Prophets and the Writings. 2 Isaiah 32:1-2 3 E.g., Isaiah 52:15- 53:12; Daniel 9:24-26 4 Isaiah 59:20 5 Genesis 1:4 6 Yalkut on Isaiah 60; see Alfred Edersheim. The life and Times of Jesus the Messiah (Wm. B. Eerdmans 1977) p. 728. 7 Sanhedrin 99a; Berachot 34b; Shabbat 63a 8 Bereshit Rabbati 133 (Isaiah 66:7) 9 Sanhedrin 98a 10 Ibid. 11 Sukkah 52b 12 Zechariah 12:10 13 Psalm 2:7 14 Genesis 3:15 15 Genesis 3:5 16 Genesis 3:15 17 See J.W. Etheridge, The Targum of Onkelos and Jonathan Ben Uzziel on the Pentateuch with the Fragments of the Jerusalem Targum from the Chaldee [hereafter referred to as Etheridge] (Katav 1968) p. 166 vote 8. This targum is commonly referred to as the Targum of Jonathan Ben Uzziel. 18 Genesis 4:1 19 See Etheridge at pp. 169-170. 20 Genesis 4:25 21 Midrash Rabbah Genesis 23:5 (22) II Samuel 7:12-13 (23) I Chronicles 22:8 (24) II Samuel 7:13-14,16 (25) I Kings 11:3-6 (26) Hosea 3:5 (6) Ezekiel 34:23-24 (7) Amos 9:12 (8) Jeremiah 23:5-6 (27) Micah 5:2 (28) Psalm 89:27,29,34-37.(29) Midrash Rabbah Shemot 19. Jewish commentators interpret the psalmic passage as Messianic. They note rightfully that the faithful witnesses in heaven are the sun and the moon mentioned in the psalm. Hence, they link it to a prophecy in the book of Jeremiah where God takes the sun, moon and stars to be witnesses before him that Israel will endure forever (Jeremiah 31:35-36). These same witnesses testify that Messiah is the first begotten of God and that He will endure forever.

(30) Psalm 2:1-2, 6-7. This warning to obey God's anointed (which is fairly translated Messiah), also here described as Son, is likewise conveyed in the Deuteronomy prophecy previously discussed in Chapter Seven, where the Messiah is described as a prophet "like unto Moses," and "whosoever will not hearken unto my words which he shall speak ... I will require it of him." (Deuteronomy 18:19) The warning also attaches to a scripture in the book of Exodus where the Messiah is revealed as the Angel of the Lord: "Behold I send an Angel before thee to keep thee in the way. ... Beware of him and obey his voice, provoke him not..." (Exodus 23:20-21) (31) Proverbs 30:4 (32) Isaiah 9:6-7 (33) Daniel 7:13 (34) Daniel 7:14 (35) Sanhedrin 97b (36) Ibid. (37) Midrash Rabbah Gen. 98:3 (38) Ibid. (39) B'reshit Rabbati, pp. 130-131; see Raphael Patai, The Messiah Texts (Wayne State Univ. Press 1979) p. 125 . [hereafter referred to as Messiah Texts] (40) Lamentations 1:2 (41) Messiah Texts at 26-27, 122-23 (42) Daniel 9:24-26 (43) Isaiah 53:/1-5.

BIBLIOGRAPHY

Gleason L. Archer, *A Survey of Old Testament Introduction*. Chicago: Moody Press, 1964. 2nd ed. 1974. 3rd ed. 1994. 608 pages. ISBN: 0802482007. A standard conservative survey, often polemical.

Raymond B. Dillard and Tremper Longman III, *An Introduction to the Old Testament*. Grand Rapids: Zondervan, 1994.

Roland K. Harrison, *Introduction to the Old Testament*. Grand Rapids: Eerdmans, 1969. 1,325 pages.

Hebrew Language

William Chomsky, *Hebrew: The Eternal Language*. Philadelphia: Jewish Publication Society, 1957.

Edward Y. Kutscher, *A History of the Hebrew language*, edited by Raphael Kutscher. Jerusalem: Magnes Press, Hebrew University, 1982. 306 pages. ISBN: 9652233978.

Henry Craik, *The Hebrew Language: Its History and Characteristics, Including Improved Renderings of Select Passages in our Authorized Translation of the Old Testament*. London: Bagster, 1860. 187 pages.

Texts

Jacob ben Hayyin, ed., *Biblia Rabbinica*: A Reprint of the 1525 Venice Edition. 4 volumes. Jerusalem: Makor Publishing, 1972. A reprint of the Rabbinic Bible originally published by Daniel Bomberg in Venice.

Aharon Dotan, ed. *Biblia Hebraica Leningradensia*, Prepared according to the Vocalization, Accents, and Masora of Aaron ben Moses ben Asher in the Leningrad Codex. Peabody, Mass: Hendrickson Publishers, 2001.

Norman H. Snaith, *Sefer Torah, Nevi'im u-Khetuvim* [title transliterated from Hebrew script]. London: British and Foreign Bible Society, 1958. Reprinted under the title The Hebrew Scriptures. ISBN: 0564000299.

Meïr Letteris, ed., *The Holy Scriptures of the Old Testament, Hebrew and English*. London: British and Foreign Bible Society, 1866. Often reprinted.

The JPS Hebrew-English Tanakh. Philadelphia: Jewish Publication Society, 1999. ISBN: 0827606567.

Hebrew-English Interlinear Editions

John R. Kohlenberger III, ed., *The NIV Interlinear Hebrew-English Old Testament*. Grand Rapids: Zondervan, 1979-85.

Concordances

John R. Kohlenberger III and James A. Swanson, *The Hebrew English Concordance to the Old Testament with the New International Version*. Grand Rapids: Zondervan, 1998. 2192 pages.

Abraham Even-Shoshan, *A New Concordance of the Old Testament*. Grand Rapids: Baker, 1989.

Lexicons

Francis Brown, Samuel R. Driver, and Charles A. Briggs, eds., *A*

Hebrew and English Lexicon of the Old Testament. Oxford: Clarendon Press, 1906. Corrected edition, 1952. Known by the abbreviation BDB. Still the standard lexicon in English.

William L. Holladay, ed., *A Concise Hebrew and Aramaic Lexicon of the Old Testament,* based on the Lexical Work of Ludwig Koehler and Walter Baumgartner. Grand Rapids: Eerdmans, 1971. 425 pages.

Wilhelm Gesenius, *Gesenius' Hebrew and Chaldee Lexicon to the Old Testament Scriptures.* Translated with additions from the author's Thesaurus and works, by S. P. Tregelles. London: Samuel Bagster & Sons, 1846.

David J. A. Clines, ed., *The Dictionary of Classical Hebrew.* 8 vols. scheduled (Sheffield Academic Press, 1993-present). The first volume 1993, vol.2 in 1995, vol. 3 in 1996, vol. 4 in 1998, vol. 5 in 2001, vol. 6 in 2003.

Hebrew and Jewish Culture

William Smith, Smith's *Bible Dictionary* (Grand Rapids, Mi.: Zondarvan, 1948)

J.I. Packer, Merril C. Tenney, William White, Jr., *Nelson's Illustrated Encyclopedia of Bible Facts* (Nashville: Thomas Nelson, 1995)

Madelene S. Miller and J. Lane Miller, *Harper's Bible Dictionary,* (New York, Harper, 1973)

Henry H. Halley, *Halley's Bible Handbook*(Grand Rapids, Mi: Zondervan, 24th)

The New Westminster Dictionary of the Bible (Philidelphia, Westminster, 1976)

NIV Compact Dictionary of the Bible, (Grand Rapids, Zondervan, 1989)

The Lion Encyclopedia of the Bible, (Tring, Lion, 1986)

Fred H. Wight, *Manners and Customs of Bible Lands* (Chicago: Moody, 1983)

Madeleine S. Miller and J. Lane Miller, *Encyclopedia of Bible Life* (New York: Harper & Brothers, 1944)

Hebrew Word Studies

James Strong, *New Strong's Concise Dictionary of the Words in the Hebrew Bible*, (Nashville, Nelson, 1995)

W. E. Vine, Merrill F. Unger, William White, *Vine's Expository Dictionary of Biblical Words*, (Nashville, Nelson, 1985)

Benjamin Davidson, *The Analytical Hebrew and Chaldee Lexicon*, (London, Samuel Bagster)

Isaac Mozeson *The Word: the Dictionary that reveals the Hebrew origin of English* (New York. S.P.I. Books, Inc.)

Ehud Ben-Yehuda, David Weinstein, *English-Hebrew Hebrew-English Dictionary*, (N.Y., Washington Square Press, Inc., 1961)

Rev. Walter W. Skeat, *A Concise Etymological Dictionary of the English* Language, (N.Y., Capricorn Books, 1963)

Ancient Languages and their Origin

John Philip Cohane *The Key*, (N.Y., Crown Publishers, 1969)

Charlton Laird *The Miracle of Language* (Greenwich Conn., Fawcett, 1953)

Giorgio Fano, *The Origins and Nature of Language*, (Bloomington

In., Indiana University Press, 1992)

Isaac.E Mozeson, *The Origin of Speeches* 2nd edition, Lightcatcher Books, Springdale,AR ISBN 0-9792618-0-5

Simple Book Resources

Ancient Hebrew Lexicon of the Bible
By Jeff A. Benner

The Ancient Hebrew Language and Alphabet
By Jeff A. Benner

The Ancient Tav
By Dr. Frank T. Seekins

Hebrew Pocket Dictionary
By Ben Yehuda

Hebrew and Chaldee Lexicon
By Friedrich Wilhelm Gesenius (1846)

Hebrew Word Pictures
By Dr. Frank T. Seekins

The New Dictionary
By Avraham Eben-Shoshan

Printed in Great Britain
by Amazon